© MCMXCVI by Barbour Publishing, Inc.

ISBN 1-58660-883-5

Cover image © PhotoDisc, Inc.

Published by Barbour Books, an imprint of Barbour Publishing, Inc., P.O. Box 719, Uhrichsville, Ohio 44683, www.barbourbooks.com

 Member of the
Evangelical Christian
Publishers Association

Printed in the United States of America.
5 4 3 2 1

1 0 1
WAYS TO SAY
"I LOVE YOU"

*S*ay it, whisper it,

or sing it,

but just make sure

you do it often.

"I love you."

2

Send flowers.
From the florist or your garden,
the essence is the same.

3

Send poetry.
From the pen of Solomon,
Elizabeth Barrett Browning, or you,
the meaning is the same.

4

Say "Will you marry me?"
You might light up the scoreboard at the stadium.

5

Or, proclaim your intentions
on a high-flying banner
(pulled by an airplane) at the beach. . . .

6

Or, broadcast your desires on tape,
spliced over a commercial
on one of her favorite prerecorded
romantic movies. . . .

7

Or, pop the question
after a treasure hunt of sorts,
with the diamond of her dreams
carefully concealed.

8

Or, propose over a candlelight
dinner at the scene of your first date
or meeting, including
an empty football stadium,
a deserted beach,
an airplane hangar—
almost anywhere.

9

Paddle your love through moonlit waters.

10

Give a gift for no reason,
except to say "I love you."

11

Compliment the love of your life often,
in private and in public.

12

Hide little gifts around the house
for your spouse.

13

Write a note to your spouse, then hide
it in a special, sure-to-be-found place.

14

Send a love note by overnight delivery.
(Write: "I just couldn't wait to say 'I love you.'")

15

Give big bear hugs.

16

Sit next to your wife
in the restaurant booth, not across from her.

17

Spend time with the one you love.
Share a simple lunch,
play board games, take a walk,
go for a bike ride (tandem, too).

18

Suggest activities you know
your spouse will enjoy
(even if you'd rather do something else).

19

Spend the first fifteen minutes
upon arriving home each day
visiting with your spouse.
Alone.

20

Treat your love to a triple-scoop ice cream cone.

21

Plan a weekend fishing or
camping trip with your spouse.
It's a chance to be together without
interruption. . .a chance
to recapture intimacy.

22

Surprise your spouse. Make the bed,
do the dishes, go grocery shopping,
shovel the sidewalk, balance the checkbook,
pick up the dry cleaning. . .
make your own love list.

Give

lingering kisses.

24

Plan a night or a weekend
at a charming bed and breakfast inn
with your spouse.

25

Tie on that apron
and give your spouse
a night off in the kitchen.

26

Sew on buttons for
your husband.

27

Wash each other's cars on a
hot summer day.
(Chase each other with the hose.)

28

Perfect your bedside manner.
Put together a care package by filling a cookie tin
with soup mix, cold tablets, throat lozenges,
magazines, and maybe a really good chocolate bar.
Tie a bright bow around it and seal with a kiss.
(The real thing will be a reward for recovery.)

29

Rent a convertible
on a beautiful summer day
and drive to the beach.

30

Start a devotional time for
just the two of you.

31

Read old love letters
(from each other!) together.

32

Walk hand in hand on a beach
at sunset. And then have a
cookout on the sand.

33

Plan a "mystery night" once a month.
Secret destinations might include
a concert, favorite or new restaurant,
or weekend getaway. Keep all the
arrangements to yourself
as long as possible
(although guessing is fun, too).

34

Re-create your first date
together.

35

Watch the sunrise together.
And then go out for breakfast.

36

Tour country roads together, by bike,
car, or horseback.
Take along a picnic lunch
(and a camera).

37

Give your chosen one a book by
a favorite author. Romantically inscribe the first page
(be sure to include the date).

Rent an old movie

to watch together on a chilly,

rainy day—under a blanket.

39

Create your own
holiday traditions.

40

Surprise your heartthrob with tickets
to his or her favorite team's game.
(Make sure the seats aren't in the
nosebleed section!)

41

Plan a service project together: volunteer
at a homeless shelter, soup kitchen, or
hospital ward. Enrich your own relationship
as you enrich the lives of others.

42

Surprise your sweetheart by
taking him or her out to lunch.

43

Telephone your true love
unexpectedly—"I just called to
say 'I love you.' "

44

Keep a thank-you jar. Throughout the year
jot down reasons why you're thankful
for your spouse and then
read them aloud on your anniversary.

45
Share with your love
your love of Jesus Christ.

46
Encourage each other's hobbies.

47
Give a small gift every day of the week
(or month) preceding a birthday
or anniversary.

48

Lie outside on a blanket
on a clear night
and watch the stars.

49

Slip a love note in his lunch sack.

50

Call a local radio station and dedicate
"your song" to the one you love.

51

Remember your wedding day.
Every now and then,
go through your wedding album
or watch your wedding
video together.

52

Remind your spouse why you
love him or her more with every year.

53

Pray for each other.

54

Have a professional photographer
take your portrait. Give yourself
(uniquely framed) to the one you love.

55

Keep a scrapbook
of your life together.

56

Plan a dream vacation.

57

Create special nonverbal signals. Three hand
squeezes might mean "I love you"; rubbing your
chin could say "Let's get out of here!"

58

Write a letter to your future mother-in-law.
Tell her how blessed you
are to marry her child.

59

Escape a dreary Saturday
over cups of cappucino.

60

Write a letter—years later—to your
mother-in-law. Thank her for raising
such a wonderful man to be your husband.

61

Plant a tree together on
your first anniversary
(or when the weather warms up).

62

Learn a new sport together.

63

Learn to play a sport
your significant other
already enjoys.

64

Enroll in a ballroom dancing class.
(There were major sparks, after all,
between Fred and Ginger.)

65

Be the first to make up. Don't let
a day end with an argument.

Remind each other

of the reasons you

fell in love.

67

Throw a surprise birthday party
for the one you love.
First, though, make sure they'll
appreciate such a gesture.

68

Make sure you look
your best when you're out
with your spouse.

69

Keep in shape. Chances are, you'll spend
more years with your spouse, and you'll
be more attractive to her or him.

70

Give your bride a day of beauty at a local spa.
(Then pour on the compliments!)

71

Comfort your spouse. Tender is the
day and night when you offer a shoulder
to cry on, a handkerchief to wipe away the tears.

72

Be a gentleman. Hold open all doors for her,
pull out (and push in) her chair, and
introduce her proudly to others.

73

Secure her future.
Make out a will after you're married.

74

Attend church and
Sunday school together.

75

Encourage your spouse to go out with friends.
Every relationship needs some
breathing room.

76

Prepare a gourmet meal together.
(The kitchen is the perfect place for
a "chemistry" lesson.)

77

Go clothes shopping with your wife.
Insist she try on many outfits.

78

Suggest her or his parents come
for a visit (or for dinner).

79

Share household
responsibilities.

80

Learn to say "I love you"
in a foreign language.

81

Share babysitting
responsibilities.

82
Speak kindly to (and of)
your spouse—always,
no matter what.

83
Call every day you're away
on a business trip.

84
Call in "well" and spend a weekday together.
Stroll through a favorite museum.
Lunch leisurely at an obscure bistro
which, unlike your love, is a well-kept secret.

85
Hold hands when going
for a walk.

86
Hold on to each other when
the going gets rough.

87
Display at work a photo
of your spouse.

88

Laugh even when your beloved
blows the punchline.

89

Laugh even when you've heard her
joke quite a few times before.

90

Smile when the woman or man
you love enters the room.

91

Make up your own nicknames
for each other.

92

Celebrate all of your spouse's
accomplishments—big or small—
with panache.

93

Decorate your home with beauty—bright colors,
flowers, music, warmth, and laughter—
and love will always be there.

94

Tape a love note to the
bathroom mirror.

95

Give a shoulder massage after a
stressful day at work or school.

96

Raise your daughter to see in her father
what a husband should be.

97

Remember the love you've shared all year.
Give your spouse a Christmas tree
ornament that brings back a special memory.

98

Raise your son to aspire to win a
woman like his mother.

99

Remember that your marriage
vows were made before God.

100

Retreat at the end of each year
to a mountain cabin
(or anywhere away from civilization).
Beside a roaring fire assess the
past year together.
Dream dreams
for the year ahead.

101

Return to the place you spent your
honeymoon. Renew your love for each other.